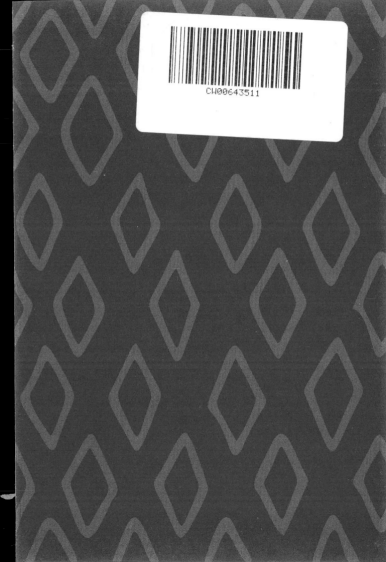

CW00643511

Little
SPONTANEOUS
ADVENTURES

How to break routine
and enjoy something new
— *every day* —

Amber Reid

summersdale

LITTLE SPONTANEOUS ADVENTURES

An Hachette UK Company
www.hachette.co.uk

Summersdale Publishers Ltd
Part of Octopus Publishing Group Limited
Carmelite House
50 Victoria Embankment
LONDON
EC4Y 0DZ
UK

www.summersdale.com

Printed and bound in Malta

ISBN: 978-1-78783-249-7

Substantial discounts on bulk quantities of Summersdale books are available to corporations, professional associations and other organizations. For details contact general enquiries: telephone: +44 (0) 1243 771107 or email: enquiries@summersdale.com.

CONTENTS

Introduction

>>>> >>>> >>>> >>>> >>>> >>>> >>>> >>>> >>>> >

Do you spend too much time gazing out of a window, wondering what is beyond the horizon? Have you made a list of all the things you're going to try "one day"? Or have you simply felt stuck in a rut recently? It sounds as though you need to go adventuring.

It's true, some adventures need lots of planning and preparation. They need forethought and test runs and all sorts of equipment! There are some adventures that can only happen once every few years because they are so big. But not little spontaneous adventures. Little spontaneous adventures can happen every day – sometimes even several times a day! They are five breath-taking minutes before breakfast, a moment of beauty at lunchtime or an unplanned jaunt after dark.

It's through these small adventures that you break routine and breathe fresh air into your life. They feed the soul. This little book is bursting with them, offering a new idea every time you turn the page.

Stop waiting for adventure to come to you. Go out and seek it.

Little
ADVENTURES

These little magic moments are
the perfect size to squeeze into
your daily routine: take a passing
chance, seize a fleeting moment
and try something new today.

TELL ME, WHAT IS IT
YOU PLAN TO DO WITH
YOUR ONE WILD AND
PRECIOUS LIFE?

MARY OLIVER

Challenge yourself to a
lunchtime scavenger hunt. Find
something beautiful, something
wild, something that smells good
and something that's perfectly
imperfect. Take a photo, sketch
or write a short description
of the things that you find.

Set your alarm for daybreak
and watch the sunrise. Take
note of the delicate colours
spreading across the sky and the
stillness around you. Listen
for the dawn chorus and try to
distinguish the different types
of birdsong that you can hear.

TRYING SOMETHING
NEW WILL TEACH
YOU SOMETHING NEW.

Pack a picnic to enjoy in your lunch hour. Distinguish it from an everyday packed lunch by including picnic foods such as pies, tarts, pickled goods and seasonal fruits. Bring a blanket to sit on — or a large jacket will do — and pick the most beautiful spot around to eat your lunch.

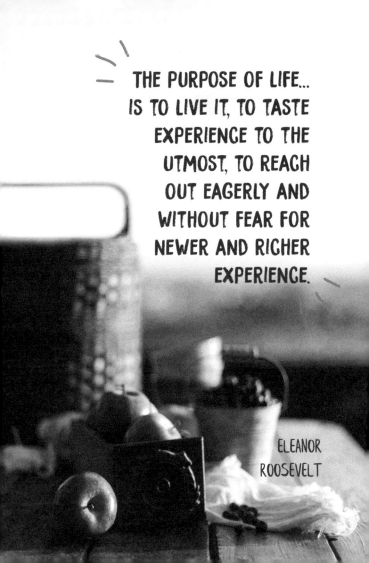

THE PURPOSE OF LIFE...
IS TO LIVE IT, TO TASTE
EXPERIENCE TO THE
UTMOST, TO REACH
OUT EAGERLY AND
WITHOUT FEAR FOR
NEWER AND RICHER
EXPERIENCE.

ELEANOR
ROOSEVELT

Go outside and feel the grass underneath your bare feet. Whether you step onto your lawn or travel to a local green spot, connecting with nature will calm your mind and refresh your spirit.

Walk a different route to work this morning. Notice the little details of your fresh surroundings such as an interesting plant in someone's front garden, an old advert still painted on the side of a wall or a coffee shop you've not passed before.

Salute the sun. Take your yoga mat to a local green space, or even your own back garden, and position yourself so the sun is on your face. Complete a sun salutation or simply move through some of your favourite positions. Let your self-consciousness fall away and enjoy the feeling of stretching your body among the elements.

If you enjoy a little weekday snack or drink, then try swapping out your old favourite for something new. You could make this into a challenge, treating yourself to new delights until you've tried everything new in your local area — then, if you like, you can return to the old comforts, having broken out of your routine.

Spread a little goodness in the world and pick up three items of waste from the street today. Some adventures are fights against unseen foes, such as the forces that have led to our beautiful world overflowing with waste. Once you have picked up the litter — using gloves if you prefer — dispose of it appropriately, recycling all the materials that you can.

Travel around the world in your lunchbreak. Prepare a traditional lunch from a different country from a Japanese bento box to an Argentinian empanada. Most ingredients will be easily sourced from your local supermarket, but try to source the harder-to-find ingredients from a local speciality store instead of ordering online — you may have two adventures in one and find a new favourite store.

Paint small rocks with images
or patterns and hide them
around your local area. There
is the potential for two
adventures with this activity
— an idle lunchbreak spent
painting and the reverse
treasure hunt of secreting
the rocks around your area.

GO AND CATCH
A FALLING STAR.

John Donne

Find a green space and try to
cartwheel or handstand. Ask a
friend to support you if you're
not comfortable — in fact, it
could be even more fun if there
are two of you, and you may feel
less self-conscious in a group.
Relive your youthful days by
tumbling and going upside down!

Dogs are little invitations to adventure. Dog owners, you may have fallen into a routine, going out to the same trusty dog-walking spots and only venturing to new locations at the weekend. The next time you step out with your faithful companion, take a left instead of the usual right, or walk to the park that's five minutes further. Notice the joy and curiosity your dog takes in its new surroundings and employ a little of the same yourself.

Turn rainy days into
"go-out-and-do-it" days. Pack
some waterproof shoes and a
large raincoat and go splashing
in puddles on your lunchbreak.
Check your surroundings for
innocent bystanders and then
give it everything you've got:
big swinging kicks, springy
hops and heavy two-footed jumps.

Remember when lunchtime was playtime? Reignite that spark by playing a board game or card game with your friends. There are plenty of modern board games that are easily transportable and can be completed in under an hour.

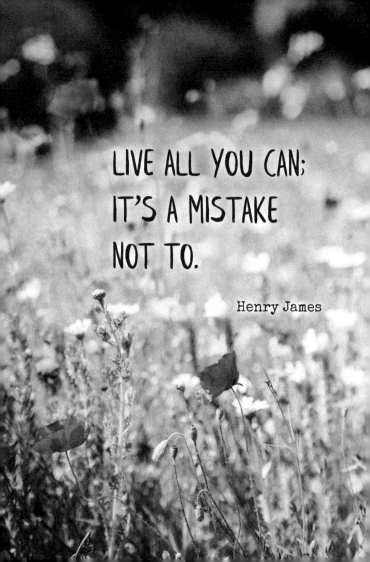

LIVE ALL YOU CAN;
IT'S A MISTAKE
NOT TO.

Henry James

Keep a lunchtime wildlife diary. It will help you notice the extraordinary in the commonplace. Fill your notebook with lists: lists of the flowers that blossom and the leaves that fall, of the birds that flit on the horizon or collect nesting material, and of the insects that bustle around or hover sleepily.

Take an hour-long summer holiday. Invite a group of friends or colleagues to play summer games, such as Frisbee, treat yourself to an ice cream and, finally, set your alarm and stretch out in the warm sunlight for a ten-minute nap.

Seek seasonal wonders:
search for natural beauties such
as springtime blossom, summer
wildflowers, autumn leaves in
fall and frozen pools in winter.

OUR BRIGHTEST BLAZES
OF GLADNESS ARE
COMMONLY KINDLED
BY UNEXPECTED
SPARKS.

SAMUEL JOHNSON

Don't pack lunch on market days. Wander down to your nearest market — travel to one if you have access to transport — and treat yourself to something from one of the stalls. Take your time perusing the available wares and say yes to every sample offered. Dip, lick, sip and nibble your way around until you finally select your perfect lunch.

Those living, working or learning near a university have a wealth of free and inexpensive entertainment available to them. Look online for your local university's arts schedules and attend a lunchtime recital or visit a student art exhibition.

There are some charity initiatives that allow you to donate a small portion of your time. Perhaps you could spend one lunch a month meeting with an older person who seeks companionship or lending a hand to someone who needs a little help around the house.

Learning new things will
open up doors in your mind.
Watch a lecture online — there
are plenty available for
free — on a topic you know
nothing about. There is an
entire universe out there, by
learning something new you'll
have traversed a little more
of it than you had yesterday.

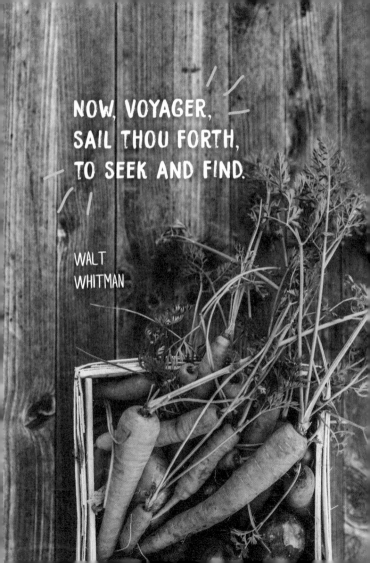

NOW, VOYAGER,
SAIL THOU FORTH,
TO SEEK AND FIND.

WALT
WHITMAN

Buy only the ugly and nearly out-of-date fruit and veg at your local corner shop or supermarket. Take them home for dinner. Pies are the best dish for ugly veg as by the time they've been chopped, flavoured, covered in pastry and baked for an hour you'll have forgotten what they ever looked like. The only thing you'll notice is just how darn delicious they are.

Buy googly eyes and place them on a few strategic items around the house, school or office. You'll be surprised how the ordinary can transform into the absurd with just a googly eye or two! In the right environment you'll bring joy to yourself and others around you. (Avoid attaching eyes to: your loved ones' expensive items, your boss's files for an important meeting or your best friend's wedding cake.)

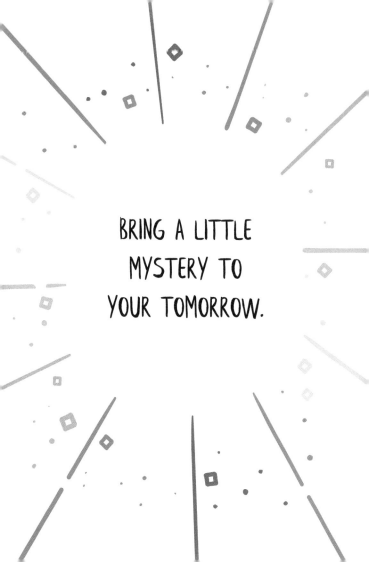

BRING A LITTLE
MYSTERY TO
YOUR TOMORROW.

Go on a date with your love.
Perhaps you'll meet for a
swift coffee, maybe you both
have time to meet at home and
share a meal or perhaps all
you can spare is five minutes
to embrace. Any time spent
together breaking your daily
routine is worthwhile.

LISTEN: THERE'S A HELL OF A GOOD UNIVERSE NEXT DOOR; LET'S GO.

E. E. CUMMINGS

Book an exercise class during your lunchbreak and get your heart racing. Many local gyms offer short classes designed to slip into your daily schedule. Those in need of a budget-conscious adventure can follow an online tutorial or go for a short, sharp run.

Does your lunch contain
enough whimsy? Kiss goodbye
to dull everyday lunches
with this microwave treat
challenge. Make a chocolate
mug cake or Mexican corn in the
microwave and enjoy a little
oasis of cooking creativity.

Open your own secret lunchtime cinema for friends and colleagues, complete with popcorn. Set up a projector or adapt your phone into a projector and watch short films. Consider classics of the silver screen such as Chaplin or Laurel and Hardy or old animated shorts.

Books are windows into new universes. Spread love among your fellow travellers by going to your local library and slipping positive notes in some of the books. A simple "have a nice day" will suffice, or perhaps you could leave a comment about how much you enjoyed a particular character or chapter.

MIX A LITTLE
FOOLISHNESS WITH YOUR
SERIOUS PLANS. IT IS
LOVELY TO BE SILLY AT
THE RIGHT MOMENT.

HORACE

Film one second a day, every day. Focus your camera on any moment throughout the day that takes your fancy, or capture your favourite moment and create a highlight reel.

Start a weekday with a luxurious breakfast. Have some fun with huevos rancheros or pancakes topped with fresh fruit. Go all out with a virgin mimosa — orange juice topped with sour lemonade — served in a fluted glass. If this little adventure appeals to you but you simply can't spare the time, prepare some overnight oats and top with chopped fruit in the morning — it's delicious and takes no time out of your morning routine.

FIRST YOU
HAVE A DREAM,
THEN YOU HAVE A
DREAM COME TRUE.

Writing a love letter is like
falling in love all over again.
Write to your love and tell them
all the ways you adore them,
how you feel when you see them
and how wonderful they are.

IT'S BETTER TO WEAR
OUT THAN TO RUST OUT.

MARY ANN
SHADD CARY

Create a riddle trail for a friend or colleague. Hide clues around the local area during your lunch hour and see if they can solve it during theirs. If your locale isn't suited to hiding physical clues then you could control the riddle trail via phone message, or join your friend on the trail and hand them the next clue when they hit on the solution.

Find connection through learning. Run a skill swap with your friends or colleagues. You can exchange marketable skills, such as a beginner's guide to Photoshop or learning the basics of analyzing quantative information. This is a good way to strengthen your and your team's professional skills. Or you could have a little fun with it and swap hobby skills, such as origami or chess, or teach each other phrases in a foreign language.

Wake up early and walk in the
pale morning light to a local
café for a fancier-than-normal
breakfast. Pretend for a moment
that you're on holiday and that
the day will hold countless
unknown adventures — and
then see how that transforms
your familiar surroundings
into something more beautiful
and a little unknown.

HAPPINESS IS
A WORTHWHILE
PURSUIT.

Evening
ADVENTURES

As our longest period of free time on a workday, the evening holds so much potential. Why waste it on watching TV or scrolling through social media? Make yourself a promise to spend at least one evening a week having a new adventure.

IF YOU THINK
ADVENTURE IS
DANGEROUS,
TRY ROUTINE -
IT'S LETHAL.

PAULO COELHO

The stars arrive early during winter. Wrap up warm and head outside to a local area that is free of light pollution. Gaze at the stars, looking for constellations that you recognize and trying to spot any unfamiliar sights. Check online to learn whether there are any upcoming celestial events such as large full moons, satellites or meteor showers.

Take advantage of the lingering
sunshine during summer and
invite a loved one to come and
watch the sunset with you.
The beauty of a setting sun
can transform any landscape
so you could set out to watch
as many different sunsets as
possible during the summer,
including: a cityscape, a
lakeside, a hilltop or the beach.

SEEK ADVENTURE,
FIND FREEDOM.

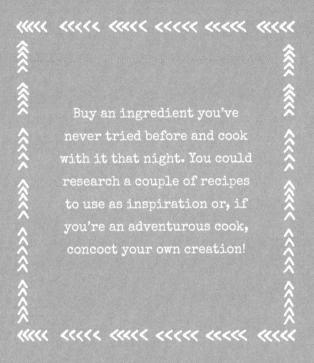

Buy an ingredient you've never tried before and cook with it that night. You could research a couple of recipes to use as inspiration or, if you're an adventurous cook, concoct your own creation!

THE FEARS ARE PAPER
TIGERS. YOU CAN DO
ANYTHING YOU
DECIDE TO DO.

Amelia Earhart

Attend an evening of local entertainment, tonight. Search online for what's on — you might find a comedy night, live music playing at a pub or bar or a community theatre performance. If you live in a quieter area you may need to book a ticket for the soonest available night. Do it — you're still being spontaneous.

Forage for food on public land or in your own garden. If you're not a practised forager then leave the riskier plants, like mushrooms, to the experts. Focus instead on edible plants such as bramble fruits, or ingredients that can be brewed into tea such as dandelion root or nettle leaf.

Find a quiet space where you won't be disturbed and listen to a new album all the way through. If possible — and if you won't doze off — close your eyes so you can focus your senses on experiencing the music. Really zero in on the details of each song like the emotion in the singer's voice, the timbre of the instruments, the wit of the lyrics, and let yourself sail away to the music.

Don't let your life become a checklist, living from one task to the next. Tonight, don't go straight home after work. Take a walk down a pretty street or along a river or canal if possible — or anywhere you fancy! Take the time for leisure before you start on your life admin or usual evening routine.

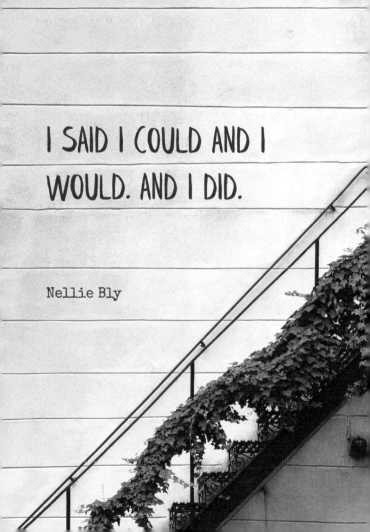

I SAID I COULD AND I
WOULD. AND I DID.

Nellie Bly

Hold a "never wear" party.
Invite your friends and tell
them to wear something they
own but never wear. This gives
everyone the chance to dust
off that one daring outfit
that they rarely find the
opportunity to wear, and you can
enjoy all the fun of a costume
party with none of the cost.

"Flower bomb" your local area. Flower bombing is the act of scattering easy-to-grow wildflower seeds on untended public spaces, to transform ugly spaces into beautiful ones and improve the habitat for bees and insects. Always check that the area you plan to flower bomb is not protected or a fragile ecosystem.

I CAN'T WAIT
TO SEE
WHAT YOU DO.

Buy a pack of sparklers or glowsticks and step outside to play in the dark. The night is beautiful already — think how it will be lit up with golden sparks or laced with neon.

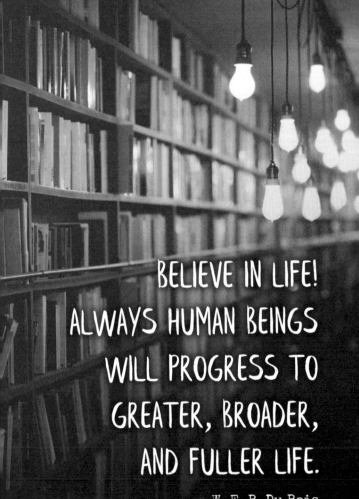

BELIEVE IN LIFE!
ALWAYS HUMAN BEINGS
WILL PROGRESS TO
GREATER, BROADER,
AND FULLER LIFE.

W. E. B. Du Bois

Take yourself out on a date. Go
to that eatery that you've been
meaning to try or a favourite
restaurant that you've not been
to in a while. Take a book or
download an episode to watch
while you're eating if you're
not comfortable simply sitting
— although consider putting
the entertainment aside when
your food arrives so you can
enjoy your meal mindfully.

Give yourself a hand and foot massage in the evening. Our hands and feet are some of our hardest-working body parts and we give them so little love in return. Gently rub hand or foot cream in (avoiding between your toes) or look up some simple massage techniques online.

Invite a friend over for a midweek sleepover. This is your official permission to eat pizza, watch bad films and stay up past midnight talking about everything and nothing. You could even have a midnight feast — we won't tell if you won't.

Run away from home for the night. Pack your bag and book yourself into a nearby Airbnb or motel. If you live in a busy house, if you're often a caretaker of others or if your home isn't the source of comfort you'd like it to be right now, this tip is especially for you. Tonight is a no-chore, no-responsibility, bath, boxset and book night.

IF YOU OBEY ALL THE RULES, YOU MISS ALL THE FUN.

Katharine Hepburn

Unplug all your electronics
for the evening and switch off
your devices. That's all there
is to it — how you entertain
yourself is part of the
challenge. Do you want to take
the opportunity to relax, to be
productive or even get creative?

Create a messaging group for
a select few friends and loved
ones, and set a theme or issue
a challenge. This could be
something as simple as a "name
that song" group for your fellow
music lovers, or challenging
your pals to send a photo of
their weirdest find in an
antique store. These groups
will add an element of fun to
your conversations, allowing
you to connect and be silly.

GOOD THINGS COME
TO THOSE WHO
SEEK THEM.

Join in on a night run or night cycle and enjoy the slightly topsy-turvy feeling of doing an activity that usually happens in the daytime, at night. Night races, rallies and rides come with a buzz from the crowd and the adrenaline of exercising.

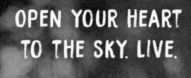

OPEN YOUR HEART
TO THE SKY. LIVE.

ADAM GNADE

Sleep outside on a weeknight,
even if it's only in your own
garden. Reset back to your
natural rhythms by going to
bed as twilight falls, letting
the dimming light pull you
down into sleep, and by getting
up at first light, waking as
the natural world wakes.

Attend a "lates" event at your local museum or zoo. You'll feel like you've snuck in after hours, perhaps fulfilling a classic childhood wish. Isn't seeing a slice of history or nature with your own eyes better than another evening in front of the TV?

Drop in on a friend or relative
on the way home from work.
Don't stay long — stick to the
duration of one hot drink
or half an hour. You'll both
benefit from the connection of
talking face to face and still
have time to yourself to relax.

The evenings are for romancing.
Tell your lover that their
chores are cancelled, unplug
the TV, dim the lights and
settle down for sweet kisses.

AND TRULY, I REITERATE...
NOTHING'S SMALL!
NO LILY-MUFFLED HUM
OF A SUMMER-BEE,
BUT FINDS SOME
COUPLING WITH THE
SPINNING STARS.

Elizabeth
Barrett
Browning

Collect your spare change in a jar and when it's full, go to an arcade. Play, play and play some more, until all your coins are spent, your thumbs are sore and your arms are full of tickets.

Don't let blustery weather drive you indoors. Go outside to your nearest open green space and fly a kite. You'll need a buddy to help you launch it, and it may take a few tries, but when it flies, oh how it flies.

Take the scientific approach to life: experiment. Recall the classic kitchen experiments of childhood such as the baking soda and vinegar volcano or attempting to mix oil and washing up liquid. What else can you try? Conduct your own experiments or look online for inspiration.

Swap a quiet night in for shivers down your spine and cold fingers on the back of your neck. Sign up for a ghost tour of your local area. No one is ever more than a few miles from a haunted house or two. Join the tour alone if you dare, or attend with a friend so you'll have a hand to cling to.

WARM, EAGER, LIVING
LIFE — TO BE ROOTED
IN LIFE — TO LEARN,
TO DESIRE TO KNOW,
TO FEEL, TO THINK,
TO ACT. THAT IS
WHAT I WANT.

Katherine Mansfield

Pack your swimming costume and a towel with your lunch today and go for a swim on your way home. If you live or work near the beach then you should swim in the sea — salt water is good for your skin and the sea is free!

If you're a "do something, all the time" person then you need an adventure that will help you unwind. Tonight when you get home, change into your comfiest clothes and curl up with a mug of something warm. Lounge for as long as you're physically able, giving your mind and body the break they deserve.

If your trouble is that you do too little at the end of your day then you need to inject a bit of "something" into your evening. Inviting friends to kick a ball or throw a Frisbee for an hour is an inexpensive way to add a little fun to your life. For those who cannot bear the word "sport", a walk around a public green space with a friend will achieve the same result.

Mix two parts flour to one part salt and one part water to make salt dough. This thick mix acts much like clay. You can model and mould any shape you want, from serious attempts at improving your art skills to a lighthearted sculpting session. Once you're finished simply gather the dough back into a ball and freeze for later use.

EVERY SEASON IS
LIKEABLE, AND WET
DAYS AND FINE, RED
WINE AND WHITE,
COMPANY AND SOLITUDE.

VIRGINIA WOOLF

Buy yourself flowers. There need be no occasion. Buy yourself flowers because you're sad. Buy yourself flowers in congratulations. Buy yourself flowers because you deserve something beautiful in your life today.

Humans may start to slow down in the evenings but many in the animal kingdom are just getting started. Wait for twilight and watch for a murmeration of starlings, flitting bats or other wildlife native to your area.

THERE IS NO
BETTER MOMENT
TO START
THAN NOW.

A long commute can lead
to a person seeing a lot of
the world from a window
without ever experiencing
it. During your next journey,
stop before you get home and
visit somewhere new. You may
discover something wonderful,
such as an independent cinema
or an open mic night.

FOOTPRINTS ON THE SANDS OF TIME ARE NOT MADE BY SITTING DOWN.

ENGLISH PROVERB

Make the dinner you dreamed of as a child. It may be a dinner made entirely of candies or of nuggets shaped like dinosaurs, perhaps eaten in front of the TV, or up a tree. Let your childhood self's imagination be the limit.

Go to a nightclub on a weekday
and dance the night away. Dance
until your feet hurt and the
sweat shimmers on your brow
and all the cares of the day have
been left on the dancefloor.

BBQ food is often reserved for special occasions and weekends, but not tonight. Tonight you are cooking your dinner on the BBQ. Don't worry if it's winter, just wrap up tight and warm yourself by the coals.

TODAY IS A
BLANK PAGE –
WHAT WILL
YOU WRITE?

Big ADVENTURES

Take a longer break from routine and get out into the beautiful wide world with one of these larger adventures. They are still small enough that you can slip them into the weekend whenever excitement calls to you.

Some of the adventures listed in this chapter can be dangerous. Only opt to do the activities that are within your physical means, and always research fully before trying anything new.

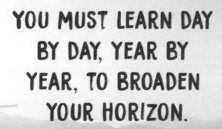

YOU MUST LEARN DAY
BY DAY, YEAR BY
YEAR, TO BROADEN
YOUR HORIZON.

ETHEL BARRYMORE

Pick a town or beauty spot that
you have never visited and that
is at least one hour's distance
from you — and then travel
there. You could research ahead
of time and select a handful
of local museums, eateries and
sites of interest to visit, or
you could simply arrive and
see where the day takes you!

Attend a free local fair or
festival. Really participate
— eat from at least one food
vendor, try one activity and
treat yourself to an item from
a stall. Dress up according to
the theme or occasion, even if
it's just a summery outfit.

SEIZE LIFE BY
THE FISTFUL.

Throw a "party under the stars". Fill your garden with candles, cook a big pot of food and invite friends over for an evening of music and dancing. If you don't have access to a garden, take a blanket, some cushions and lots of camping lights or battery-powered fairy lights to a local green space.

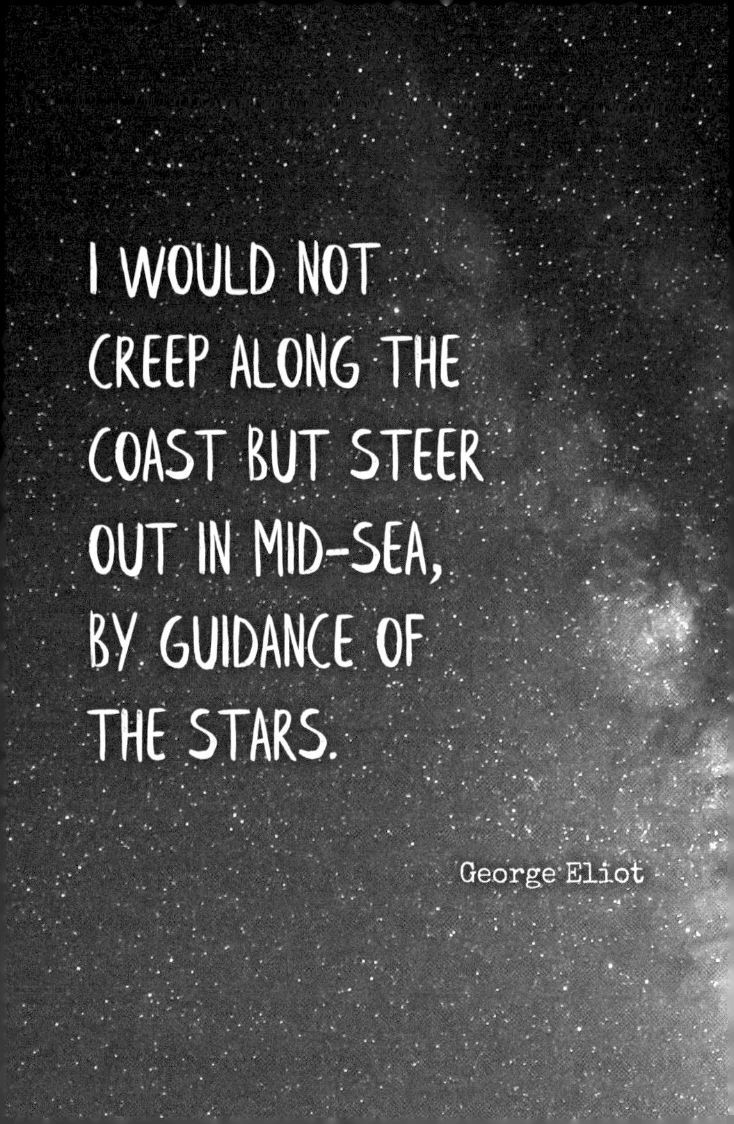

I WOULD NOT
CREEP ALONG THE
COAST BUT STEER
OUT IN MID-SEA,
BY GUIDANCE OF
THE STARS.

George Eliot

Create a "sketch diary".
Carry a notepad with you for the
day and draw everything you see
of interest, whether it be the
people you pass, architectural
features or a street performer.
You don't need fancy supplies —
just a pencil and notepad will
do. You'll be more mindful of
the beauty and wonder around
you, and at the end of the day
you'll have a unique memento.

Those who live by a body of water may notice tourist attractions such as pedal boats, punts or rowboats on offer. Don't let tourists have all the fun. Call on a friend to come with you for a little water-based adventure. The world moves differently when you're afloat — why not see life in a new way for a while?

Practise radical kindness for the whole weekend. Radical kindness is the act of attempting to understand and empathize with everyone you encounter. This means brushing away niggling annoyance with people on the street, not engaging in arguments with loved ones and finding a connection with those different to ourselves.

Make a "love map" of your local area. Ask each of your locally-based friends and loved ones for their favourite place in the area and create a map of their recommendations. If you have a flair for the artistic you could illustrate it. Take a "love tour" using the map, or keep it on hand when you want to plan a trip.

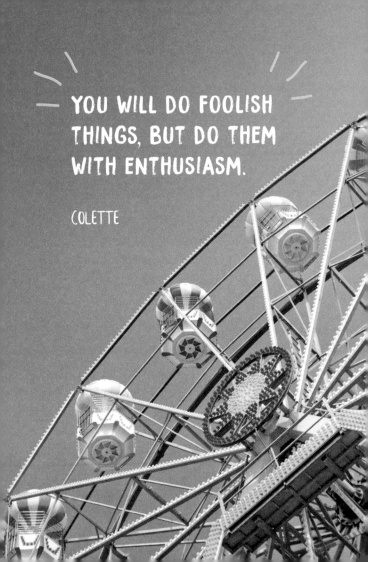

YOU WILL DO FOOLISH
THINGS, BUT DO THEM
WITH ENTHUSIASM.

COLETTE

Construct a Rube Goldberg machine — a deliberately complicated contraption that creates a chain reaction to perform a simple task. This is the perfect spontaneous adventure for a rainy day — using items from only around your home will be a fun creative challenge.

Try magnet fishing. This adventure needs a little preparation: you'll need to purchase a strong magnet, strong and flexible rope and protective gloves. Seek permission from the person who owns the river or lake you're hoping to fish in. This prep is all worth it: magnet fishing is the perfect activity for lovers of treasure hunting and oddities as you'll find lost keys, jewellery, locked boxes and maybe even a mystery or two.

SWAP "WHAT IF
I CAN'T?" FOR
"WHAT IF I CAN?"

Forge a deeper connection
with your favourite artist by
travelling to a place that is
connected to them. This could
be somewhere depicted in their
art, whether song, book, film
or painting, the location that
they created their greatest work
or a site that acted as a muse.

LIFE IS NOT
A SPECTATOR
SPORT.

JACKIE ROBINSON

Hunt for ancient ruins and old architecture in your local area. Look online or at your local library or records centre for old maps and surveys, then visit the sites you find of interest and learn more about their history. Satellite photos can show you that areas that you may have assumed were lumps and bumps in the countryside are actually the outlines of ancient forts and buildings.

Make a miniature book —
design the cover, cut the pages
and fill them with whatever
you'd like, whether it's your
favourite poem, song or a diary
entry exploring one of your
favourite days. Or perhaps you
could fill it with fragments
of your day, such as pressed
flowers, and beautiful items,
such as striking photographs,
printed paper or scraps
of interesting cloth.

Challenge your friends to
each make a three-minute film
using their camera phones,
on a topic of your choice.
Download a free or cheap app
to edit the film and add music
and filters if you like. Hold
a grand premiere where you
screen all of the films. Part of
the fun will be seeing how you
each interpreted the theme.

Go wild swimming. Slip into
cool, dark, natural waters
and let your cares float away.
Admire the shores adorned with
swaying reeds and bustling
with dragonflies in the
summer. Remember to always
research the river or lake
before you go, to ensure you
are a strong enough swimmer.

ALL THE WILD WORLD IS
BEAUTIFUL, AND IT MATTERS
BUT LITTLE WHERE WE GO,
TO HIGHLANDS OR LOWLANDS,
WOODS OR PLAINS... DOWN
AMONG THE CRYSTALS OF
WAVES OR HIGH IN A BALLOON
IN THE SKY.

John Muir

Randomize your day.
Write down three places you'd
like to visit, three foods
you'd like to eat and three
outfits you'd like to wear
on individual bits of paper.
Fold them and shuffle them by
group, then draw one piece
of paper from each group. The
resulting combination is
now your plan for the day!

Get up early and visit a market
you've never been to before.
This may be a second-hand
market, a farmers' market, a
collection of artisan makers
or a traditional flea market
— or any other kind that takes
your fancy! Take a little pocket
money and enjoy the wares.

THE BEST ADVENTURES
START WHERE YOU
LEAST EXPECT THEM.

Visit a nearby (or nearish) natural phenomenon such as a waterfall, giant tree, oddly stacked rock or whirlpool. Nothing truly matches up to nature at its weirdest.

LIFE IS EITHER A DARING
ADVENTURE OR NOTHING.

HELLEN KELLER

Explore an abandoned building.
Note that you should not
enter buildings that have
been locked up and blocked
from public entry. Look for a
tumbledown bothy, an abandoned
church or a ruined castle.

Create a feast for your loved ones, or perhaps just for yourself. Select one or more recipes that you have always wanted to taste but have skipped over in the past because they are long, or complicated, or both. Listen to music or watch an old film while you cook and dedicate the day to nourishing yourself in the most delicious way.

Lie on a blanket and gaze up at the clouds above. Note the shapes you see, the animals and ships that melt into castles and monsters. Tell yourself stories about what you see and write the best ones down in a cloud diary.

Revisit the same beauty spot
once per season and note how it
changes. Will you find beauty
in each season, from the frozen
winter to the hazy summer?
Look for the details — the buds
and the berries, the different
wildlife, even how the sky looks.

EXPERIENCE IS
NEVER LIMITED AND
IT IS NEVER COMPLETE.

HENRY JAMES

Go to the strangest museum you can find. Search online for a directory of museums in your local area or go to a local information centre. Humans are wonderful, quirky creatures and you'll soon discover how many oddities they have taken an interest in, from buttons to pencils to sex.

Celebrate a "national day of".
These days often pass us by, but
why not throw yourself into
celebrating one? Whether it's
about friendship, poetry, acorns,
or golf, a day of festivity is
always a good day. Decorate, make
or buy themed food and celebrate!

WHICH ROAD
WILL YOU TRAVEL
DOWN TODAY?

Mark the passing of the year in a way that's deeply connected to the world's natural rhythms. Celebrate the March and September equinoxes, the only two times during the year when the sun sits above the equator line, and the June and December solstices, each marking the longest and shortest days for the northern and southern hemispheres. You could host or attend a bonfire, plant a new tree or create homemade decorations to mark the occasion.

LIVE OUT OF
YOUR IMAGINATION,
NOT YOUR HISTORY.

Stephen Covey

Make your own bread. Soda bread, cornbread and flatbread are all good options for beginner bakers and there are plenty of recipes available online or at your local library. There is a unique pleasure in making food from scratch and then eating your creation.

Go back to school for the weekend. Once you are sucked into the steady thrum of everyday life, a weekend away at a course or retreat is a rare and special treat. There are plenty available, from writers' retreats to art courses to running camps and yoga festivals.

Make a zine on any topic.
A true zine is a combination of
handwritten, illustrated and
cut-out-and-stick designs,
photocopied and stapled
together to create a small
pamphlet. You could create
a classic fanzine on a topic
you're passionate about, or you
could use the medium for a fun
twist on a family newsletter
or an invite to a party.

Volunteer your time and do something good for a day. Perhaps you could participate in a beach clean or help out at a charity event. Maybe you could help a friend clear their garden or offer to look after their children so they can have some much-needed time to themselves.

SO THROW OFF THE
BOWLINES. SAIL AWAY FROM
THE SAFE HARBOUR. CATCH THE
TRADE WINDS IN YOUR SAILS.
EXPLORE. DREAM. DISCOVER.

SARAH FRANCES BROWN

Give back to your body. Search online for a last-minute spa deal and book it. Massages can be relatively inexpensive and widely available, or else you can book in for the full treatments and an overnight stay. Booking last minute can help you secure a discount deal.

See how much fun you can have using only the cash you have in your purse or wallet right now. Leave your cards at home and head out into the wide world for the day. You may not have much cash on you but that's all part of the adventure. Maybe that means walking for an hour to buy the best ice cream in the area, heading into a discount store to buy cheap craft materials, or even striking out into great outdoors.

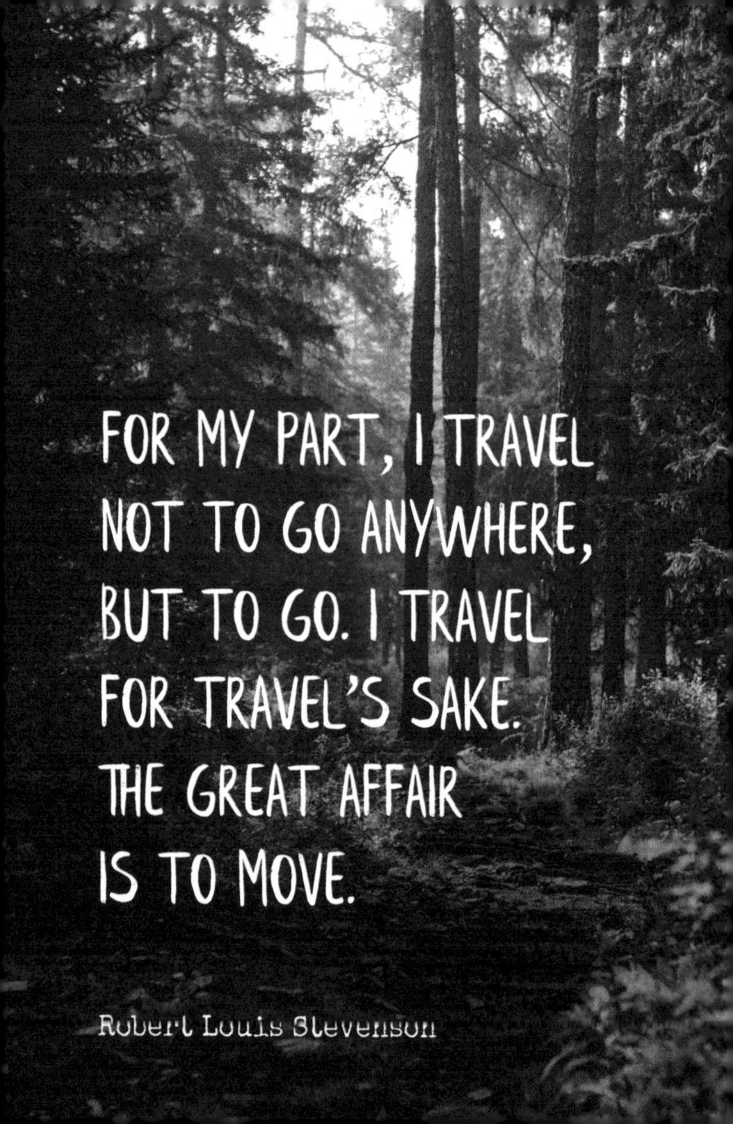

FOR MY PART, I TRAVEL
NOT TO GO ANYWHERE,
BUT TO GO. I TRAVEL
FOR TRAVEL'S SAKE.
THE GREAT AFFAIR
IS TO MOVE.

Robert Louis Stevenson

Travel to the nearest big city
and purchase last-minute
theatre tickets. Research a
couple of shows ahead of time
so you have some preferences on
your list but let the day take
you where it will — the best
thing about seeing something
you've no expectations
about is that you'll find
it much more enjoyable!

THIS IS THE MOMENT.
NOW IS THE TIME.

Travel to see a friend or loved one that you haven't seen for a good long while. Stay overnight, if they are able to host you. Visiting long-lost friends can combine the excitement of seeing somewhere new with the comfort of rekindling an old friendship.

Buy a cheap second-hand DVD and watch it. Old-school video rental may be dead but the fun and anticipation can be easily recreated in second-hand stores, which are full of cheap used DVDs. Browse the store's selection for the perfect film, and excitedly watch it later with your friends.

If you live in a town with
a port, or somewhere near
a border, slip away into
another country for the day.
Try the local cuisine, visit
a landmark or just generally
soak up the different culture.

GO WHERE YOU
FEEL MOST ALIVE.

Conclusion

>>>>> >>>>> >>>>> >>>>> >>>>> >>>>> >>>>> >>>>> >>>>> >

The future is yours to create, so make sure that you fill it with adventures of all shapes and sizes. Who knows where you will go? Who knows what you will be? There are such a lot of choices awaiting you.

Big feelings can come from little moments, so whenever you need to shake the dust off your life, pick up this book. Excitement is never far away, because there is always room for a little spontaneous adventure.

IMAGE CREDITS

If you're interested in finding out more
about our books, find us on Facebook at
Summersdale Publishers and follow
us on Twitter at @Summersdale.

www.summersdale.com